Sourdough

For Your

Food Storage

Add Nutrition and Variety

to Your Baked Goods

Millie Copper

Disclaimer

I am not a healthcare professional. I am a mom who believes that we are on the correct path for providing nutrient-dense, nourishing foods. You should do your own research and come to your own conclusions for your healthcare and nutrition, along with consulting a healthcare professional. I highly recommend contacting the Chapter Leader of your local Weston A. Price Foundation to ask about a list of healthcare providers.

This text contains affiliate links for Traditional Cooking School by GNOWFGLINS (www.TraditionalCookingSchool.com). If you make a purchase that originated from this document, I will receive a small commission. Your cost will be the same, and I greatly appreciate your support!

Table of Contents

Introduction

Is there anything better than a thick slice of bread still warm from the oven? What if that bread is not only delicious but is easier on your blood sugar and digestion and is also nutrient-rich?

One of the most difficult things when people start with bulk food storage is learning how to use raw ingredients. Buying a fifty-pound bag of white flour is an economical choice and, when properly stored, will stay fresh for years. Another economical option, with more nutrition, is purchasing wheat kernels and milling your own whole-grain flour.

By capturing and maintaining your own wild yeast sourdough starter, you can add even more nutrition and have a ready supply of yeast without needing to rely on those little commercial packages.

In 2008, when my family first started researching preparedness after a severe windstorm left us without power for a week, my awareness of our world around us changed.

Even though this was only a localized event, the entire county was affected. The first few days there wasn't even fuel available, and the grocery store was cash only with only a handful of people allowed in at a time.

While it was certainly on a smaller scale, I was reminded of images I'd seen on television of people standing in bread lines. Not a line I ever wanted to stand in. Over the next several months, we learned a lot about food storage—specifically what to store and how much.

One phrase I heard over and over was *store what you eat, eat what you store*. I'd done little baking up to that point, but I realized how much I could do with a bag of flour. Cakes, pancakes, bread, et cetera, et cetera.

Learning to bake delicious breads, muffins, and more made me feel terribly accomplished.

As our food storage efforts expanded, we purchased wheat kernels in bulk fifty-pound bags. Learning how to turn the raw wheat into tasty meals took some time and dedication. Adding in a grain mill (two actually, one electric and one manual) along with learning a variety of ways to use the wheat was my mission.

In the summer of 2009, I caught a wild sourdough starter, which opened up a whole new world of opportunities!

Not only was I making delicious bread (after some practice), but I also made snacks, breakfasts, and desserts. We loved the light tanginess of sourdough combined with the convenience and health benefits. Not needing to purchase and store commercial yeast was also very welcome.

Learning about sourdough and the wealth of ways it can be used was a huge asset to my food storage. As you read this book, I know you too will discover how this simple, primitive method can expand your food storage knowledge.

What is Sourdough?

Sourdough starter is often referred to as wild yeast. It's made simply from flour, water, and time. The wild yeast—present in the air around us and in flour—becomes your leavening agent. It's very similar to the commercial baker's yeast you purchase in the store, but also quite different.

Sourdough consists of a spontaneous fermentation process and is a very primitive form of bread leavening. It's believed to have been developed in approximately 3,000 BC in Egypt. There are several mentions of leavening in the Bible. While leavening could be any agent used to make the dough rise, such as raisins or potatoes, those little packets of yeast didn't exist until the 1800s.

Baker's yeast is domesticated from wild strains and then mass produced in a factory. It's fairly easy to use with the correct recipe and environmental temperature. The downside to commercial yeast is it's not designed to be sustainable. You use it once and then you must purchase more.

A sourdough starter is also easy to use, but it's even more forgiving with recipes and temperatures. It's also sustainable. By keeping back a small amount of starter at each use, and feeding with flour and water, your sourdough starter can be maintained for generations.

The natural occurring wild yeasts in a sourdough starter gives your dough a chance to really ferment. This breaks down hard-to-digest gluten, offering more nutrients and vitamins. Commercial yeast doesn't ferment and does little to break down the gluten. Many people who are sensitive to gluten are able to enjoy sourdough because of the fermentation process.

Sourdough starter can seem intimidating. All the feeding and care sounds like it could take too much time. What if I told you that, with just a few minutes a day, you could have a healthy and vibrant sourdough starter? It's true! Even the busiest of us can enjoy this nutritious resource.

Where Can You Find a Sourdough Starter?

If you're looking to begin nurturing your own sourdough starter, you have some excellent options!

One of the easiest is by capturing wild yeast in your own home and from your own whole grain flour. Whole wheat (or rye) flour, pure water, warmth, and time are the ingredients needed. A healthy dose of patience and optimism is also encouraged! Get detailed instructions on starting your own sourdough starter by capturing wild yeast at HomespunOasis.com/Starter.

Other options for a sourdough starter include getting a start from a sourdough-nurturing friend, asking a bakery who makes true sourdough if they sell starts, ordering a dehydrated starter from a reliable supplier such as Cultures for Health, or requesting a free (with donation) dry starter from Carl's Friends.

Maintaining a Sourdough Starter

Now that you have a sourdough starter, you may be wondering what to do with it. How do you keep it active and healthy to give you delicious baked goods?

Your hydrated starter is a living and breathing organism. It needs oxygen and food to survive. But it's also very forgiving. If you find yourself in a busy season (or on vacation) your starter is happy to rest in the refrigerator. In this section, I'll discuss the three ways I care for my sourdough starter.

During the winter, my starter is usually on the countertop in my (coolish) kitchen. I keep it covered with a flour sack towel and feed it a tablespoon or so of whole wheat flour along with a nearly equal amount of filtered well water each morning. If I think about it, or if I'm building up my starter to use for baking, I'll feed it at night too. If my kitchen was warmer (mid-70s), I'd make a point of feeding it both morning and night since heat increases the activity and it needs more food.

During the summer, I bake less and my unairconditioned home gets hot—too hot for my starter to thrive when on the counter day in and day out. I move it to the fridge and keep it in lidded mason jar.

I make a point of pulling it out of the refrigerator every week to ten days. I give it a good stir, a little flour, a little water, and then cover it with a flour sack towel and let it warm up for a few hours.

Remember, starters need not only food but oxygen. The time out of the fridge will give it a nice breath of fresh air.

The third way I care for my starter is by having a backup. I caught my starter during the summer of 2009. For months and months, years even, I babied it and made sure to stir and feed it regularly. Then life happened and I found myself in a busy time. My starter was shoved in the refrigerator and neglected.

Like, really neglected.

I went weeks and weeks without taking it out or feeding it. When I finally began to pay attention to my sourdough starter again, it looked sad. And it smelled even sadder. I wasn't sure there was anything worth saving. Miraculously, I was able to bring it back. It's now healthier and happier than ever. But I learned a valuable lesson.

Keep a backup.

I now have a small amount of frozen starter and a bit of dehydrated. "Two is one, one is none," is a good motto, even with sourdough!

What? Discard Half of My Starter?

When I was reviving my long-neglected sourdough starter, I tossed out all but about a tablespoon of it. Discarding half of your starter (or a portion) is a widely used method for developing a strong starter. While it may seem wasteful to discard extra starter, maintaining a large amount for infrequent baking would use a lot of flour over time.

After your new or rehydrated starter is at least a week old (and has had regular feedings) you can use the discarded starter in some recipes. All of my "Almost-Instant" recipes are great for using discarded starter, as are the ones for pizza, tortillas, and Bierock Pie.

There're also many ideas available on the internet for using discarded starter, just search: How to use discarded sourdough starter. Learn more about the why behind discarding at HomespunOasis.com/Discard.

Troubleshooting a New Sourdough Starter

When you're starting or rehydrating a sourdough starter, things may come up that you are unsure of. You should check any instructions included with your starter for their troubleshooting tips. Here's a few I've experienced.

No action: After a few days, your sourdough starter should be showing signs of life. There should be bubbles and the starter should "dome" within a few hours of feeding. If you are not seeing these, the first thing I'd check is the temperature.

Starters like it warm.

Seventies to eighties is great. During the summer, air conditioning can affect your starter. During the winter, the cold can be an issue. If your starter needs a little more warmth, try moving it to a toasty spot in your kitchen—maybe the top of the fridge or into the oven with the light on.

Note: Take it out of the oven before turning the oven on. Too much warmth will cook it.

Other warming ideas are to use a heating pad or place your starter near a piece of electronic equipment (such as a satellite receiver) or in a small cooler with a hot water bottle and a towel.

Keep it warm! And while you're keeping it warm, keep feeding it.

Still nothing but a lump of flour: The starter is warm (but not too warm), you're regularly feeding (every twelve hours) and vigorously stirring with each feeding, but there's still nothing going on. No bubbles. No doming. No action at all. If your starter is more than three days old and you aren't seeing any action, give it one final try before throwing in the towel.

Stir, stir, stir. Get lots of air in the mixture. Now add ¼ cup of pure water.

Stir like crazy again, then feed it ½ cup of whole wheat flour and give it a final vigorous stir. (Is your flour fresh? Fresh flour has enzymes and wild yeasts that old flour doesn't have.)

Cover with a coffee filter, paper towel, or cloth towel (not a solid lid or plastic wrap, you want air to get in) and put it in a warm place.

Check in 6 to 8 hours.

Discard half.

Repeat the stirring and feeding process.

Check again in 6 to 8 hours.

Look for signs of life. See anything? Either way, repeat the same discard, vigorous stirring, and less water/more flour feeding.

Check again in 6 to 8 hours.

If you had life at the last check, it should be even better now. Resume the original feeding instructions (amounts, discards, time). If there is still nothing happening, I'd toss it and start again. Either order another batch or try a different method, such as starting your own with whole wheat flour.

What's that smell? Sometimes around day three, you may notice an odd, less than pleasant smell. Almost like acetone or nail polish remover. This is common. I've found composting half of the starter and then giving a very small feeding of 2 tablespoons of whole wheat flour plus just under 2 tablespoons of water helps.

Then feed again 6 hours later (instead of the usual 12) without discarding. Use the 2 tablespoon measurements again for this feeding. Check again in 6 (or so) hours.

Did the smell improve? If so, go back to your regular 12-hour schedule with your usual amounts and composting.

If it's still strong and unpleasant, compost half and stick with 2 tablespoons for 6 hours for two more feedings. It should be fine after this.

Ewww, gross! What's that liquid? It's probably hooch. Hooch is a brown or gray liquid that gathers on top of the starter or can be a second layer in the middle (not as common).

Hooch is an indication that your starter is hungry. Either it has been too long since the last feeding or the feeding was too small for the conditions. During summer months, the starter is more active and may need a larger feeding when kept at room temperature.

I've found keeping my starter on the thick side helps cut down on the hooch. To have a thicker starter, feed more flour and less water instead of equal amounts.

If you do have hooch, it's fine. If there's a small amount, stir it in and move on. If there's a huge layer, carefully drain off the hooch before feeding. Then proceed as usual.

Caring for Your Sourdough Starter

Once your starter is rehydrated and bubbly, it will become stronger with use. For a newish starter, I recommend keeping it on the counter and continuing the twice-daily feeding schedule for at least a month.

You don't need to feed a half cup at time. Drop to maintenance levels, feeding 2 tablespoons of whole wheat flour and just under 2 tablespoons of water to keep a nice thick starter.

Feed larger amounts to build up for use. You can triple the amount at each feeding. Example: If you have a cup of starter (eyeball it, no need to measure) you can feed up to 2 cups flour and 2 cups of water without overwhelming the original starter. In 12 hours, you can triple again.

I use this method when I want to have a large baking day and need several cups of starter. And always remember to reserve at least ½ cup of starter to keep your starter going. So if I'm making a recipe that calls for 4 cups of starter, I need to build to at least 4 ½ cups: 4 cups for the recipe and ½ cup to continue to feed and nurture.

When your starter is at least four weeks old (or if you go on vacation at any time during your starter's life), you can move it to the fridge. Give it a good feeding before covering your glass jar (or bowl) with a well-fitting lid. Your starter will be fine for a week to ten days in the fridge.

Remove from the refrigerator and give it a small feeding before bringing it back to room temp. You should plan on at least two or three feedings at room temperature before using for baked goods that need a high rise (like loaves of bread).

Note: If you're going to be gone for longer than a couple of weeks, consider building up your starter and freezing or dehydrating a portion. This will ensure you will have healthy starter available.

And remember, when using your starter, you will always save at least ½ cup for future use. This is especially important! You must reserve starter to keep your starter going. Then you'll continue to feed and use it.

Sourdough does not need to be complicated. I've seen recipes and videos showing how to do the float test, stretch test, weighing all of the ingredients and more.

Does this make better bread?

I don't know! I've never bothered with anything like this. My bread and other sourdough goods are delicious and healthy.

And did I mention easy? I like easy. Anything I do must fit into my busy life, and sourdough is no exception.

Sourdough starter seems to need a few weeks or so to really get its groove. Please don't be discouraged if your first attempts are not what you envisioned. Young starters are perfect to use for items that don't require much rise. Pancakes, crepes, crackers, and tortillas are all excellent choices. My Rustic Biscuits are also very forgiving.

When you feel confident making these items, move on to bread. But again, give yourself (and your starter) grace. I made many a heavy, dense loaf before finally creating something I could be proud of. Be sure to check out my recipe for Sourdough Croutons. They are the perfect use for less than perfect loaves.

Sourdough as Part of Your Food Storage

Eat what you store. Store what you eat.

This is a motto we follow for our everyday food storage. There are many food calculators available to help figure out how much of each item you need to store.

The calculator I use suggests 400 pounds of grain (wheat, barley, rice, corn, oats, pasta) per person, per year. I agree storing several hundred pounds of grain is great. But knowing what to do with the grain is also important. If you have 400 pounds of hard red wheat, do you know how to make it edible?

Wheat kernels can be cooked and eaten as a porridge, they can be sprouted, or they can be ground into flour. Learning how to do these things now, and having the necessary supplies (such as a manual flour mill), would be essential in your time of need.

Personally, I think a fabulous use of wheat is in sourdough. And not just wheat. Rye, spelt, einkorn, cornmeal, and even oatmeal can be used in sourdough! Using a sourdough starter in your everyday life can also give you the confidence needed to use it during an emergency.

In the early days of the pandemic, the grocery stores in my area didn't even have commercial yeast available. There was a huge surge in people wanting to learn about true sourdough. The timing was right for learning something new, with many people off work or working from home.

The timing is right now too. By spending just a few minutes a day to get your sourdough starter going, you can gain valuable baking skills that can serve you well in the future. Plus, it'll give you options for those 400 pounds of grains per person.

Because of the long fermentation associated with sourdough, it is easier to digest than yeast bread, oatmeal, and other grains. The souring process breaks down the starches, making it much easier on your stomach. Many people who are sensitive to gluten are able to eat wheat-based sourdough. It also has a lower glycemic index, which may be kinder to blood sugars.

Note: If you have a gluten-sensitivity or blood sugar issues, you should proceed with caution and consult your physician. You could also make a gluten-free sourdough, which is made with a gluten-free starter and gluten-free grains. Get more gluten-free sourdough info and recipes at HomespunOasis.com/Sourdough-Resources.

Sourdough contains a variety of vitamins, minerals, and nutrients. A cup of wheat contains approximately 13 grams of protein. Though wheat contains protein, it is not considered a complete protein since it is low in lysine, an essential amino acid.

Combining wheat with a legume, which is high in lysine, creates a complete protein. Or slathering your sourdough with peanut butter, which is also high in lysine, will do the same. And, of course, a generous spread of rich, creamy butter (a complete protein since it's an animal product) means you don't need to think twice about that low lysine.

One of the many benefits of sourdough bread is that it stays fresh longer than its commercial counterpart, and even homemade bread made with commercial yeast. The lactobacilli in sourdough bread helps prevent mold, and the long ferment associated with sourdough helps prevent it from becoming stale.

It does dry out, the same way regular bread does when left exposed to the air, but when covered it will last for about five days at room temperature, a few additional days in the refrigerator, and several months frozen.

Be sure to check my French Toast recipe to give new life to bread that's a few days old. Sourdough Croutons are another excellent option to use up old bread. But if your family is like mine, they'll love the flavor so much that old sourdough bread is never a problem!

Rustic Biscuits

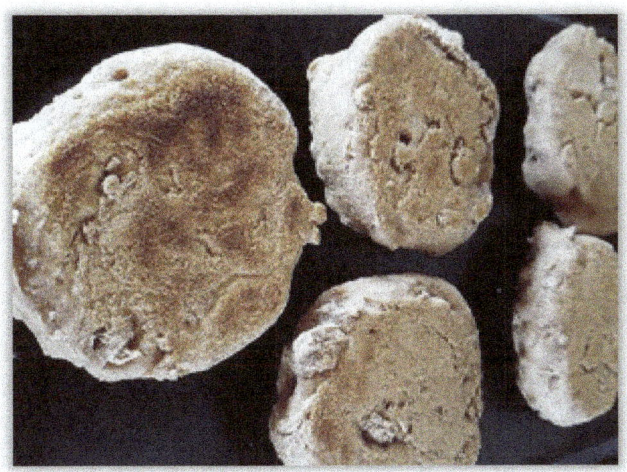

This is my favorite sourdough recipe! I can mix up a batch of this no-knead dough in minutes. Then, after it's had time to properly soak and sour (about 8 hours), a couple of flips of the wrist and I have biscuits. And the "baking" is done on the stovetop, which is fabulous for warmer months.

I'll often start the dough before bed so we can have fresh biscuits with breakfast. This recipe doubles, triples, or quadruples beautifully.

- 2 cups water
- 1 tablespoon sea salt
- 1 cup sourdough starter, fed within the last 12 hours
- 4 to 5 cups whole wheat flour, or a combination of whole wheat and white, plus additional for dusting

Combine the water, salt, and starter. Mix well.

Then add the flour, 1 cup at a time, stirring after each addition. When you reach 4 cups, stop and evaluate the dough. You want a shaggy dough—a little thicker than cake batter, but it won't be a smooth dough like when making bread. Add additional flour a few tablespoons at a time until it's a nice, thick consistency.

Now dust flour on top to cover the surface. This protects the dough and prevents a hard crust. Cover with a flour sack towel and place in a warmish spot.

About 8 hours later, your dough is ready for making biscuits!

Are you ready? If not, flip the dough and give it a quick knead to work in the flour. Sprinkle with another dusting of flour, cover with a lid (it doesn't need to be tight fitting, even your flour sack towel with a plate on top will work) and move to the fridge. The cold will slow down the souring. You can make your biscuits up to 48 hours later.

When you are ready to cook, heat a thick-bottomed skillet or griddle over medium heat.

While the skillet is heating, move the dough around to incorporate the flour on top. You're not really kneading it, just blending.

Once the flour is mixed in, pull off a chunk of dough. You will form your biscuit into a disc that looks like an English muffin and is about the same size. You can form this on a floured surface or free form using your hand. Once formed, set aside on a plate or scoot to the edge of your floured surface.

When you've used all the dough to make your biscuits, check your skillet. You want it medium to medium-high heat. With your hand about 5 inches above the skillet, you should be able to comfortably hold it there for 3 or 4 seconds.

Add a little healthy fat (butter, coconut oil, tallow, or lard) to grease the skillet. Gently place the biscuits in the skillet, leaving space between for flipping.

Set your timer for 5 minutes. When the time is up, flip the biscuits and set for another 5 minutes. Flip once again, setting your timer for 3 minutes. Remove from the heat. Repeat with any remaining biscuits.

Once all the biscuits are cooked, carefully slice in half. Return the sliced biscuits, cut side down, to the skillet to toast. This takes 3 to 5 minutes.

Enjoy slathered in butter and topped with honey or jam. Rustic Biscuits also make fabulous sandwich bread or hamburger buns. Store leftovers in a container on the counter or in the refrigerator.

Rustic Baguette or Loaf

The dough of my favorite Rustic Biscuits easily becomes a Rustic Baguette or Loaf. This dough is so flexible! Instead of one big baguette, you can make two (or maybe even three) smaller ones. Or make round cannonball loaves instead—one, two, or even three! This recipe doubles, triples, or quadruples beautifully.

- 2 cups water
- 1 tablespoon sea salt
- 1 cup sourdough starter, fed within the last 12 hours
- 4 to 5 cups whole wheat flour, or a combination of whole wheat and white, plus additional for dusting

Combine the water, salt, and starter. Mix well.

Then add the flour, 1 cup at a time, stirring after each addition. When you reach 4 cups, stop and evaluate the dough. You want a shaggy dough—a little thicker than cake batter, but it won't be a smooth dough like when making bread. Add additional flour a few tablespoons at a time until it's a nice, thick consistency.

Now dust flour on top to cover the surface. This protects the dough and prevents a hard crust. Cover with a flour sack towel and place in a warmish spot.

About 8 hours later, your dough is ready!

Are you ready? If not, flip the dough and give it a quick knead to work in the flour. Sprinkle with another dusting of flour, cover with a lid (it doesn't need to be tight fitting, even your flour sack towel with a plate on top will work) and move to the fridge. The cold will slow down the souring. You can make your bread up to 48 hours later.

Preheat your oven to 400°. Put a baking sheet or baking stone in the oven to heat at the same time.

Place a sheet of parchment paper on the table and dust with flour. Using your freshly washed hands, plop the dough on the parchment paper. Move the dough around, folding it a few times to incorporate the flour on top. You're not really kneading it, just blending. Once the flour is mixed in, evaluate your dough.

This is something that you'll get better at with experience.

Is it thick and heavy? If so, you'll want to form your baguette, loaf, or cannon ball now and then let it rest and rise for 20 minutes while the oven heats.

Is it thin and wanting to spread? If it's on the thin side and not holding its shape, you don't want to waste any time getting it in the oven. Skip the 20-minute rise. You want it in the oven and starting to rise in there. Quickly form into baguettes or loaves and get it ready to move to the oven. You can try a cannonball with a thin dough, but expect it to be more flat than round. It'll still be delicious!

Whether hustling to the oven or giving it a 20-minute rest, put a few slashes in the top immediately before moving to the oven. Slide the formed loaf from the parchment paper onto the heated baking sheet or stone.

Baking time varies depending on the wetness of the dough and whether you made a baguette, loaf, or cannonball. Smaller loaves will take around 20 minutes, where big cannonball loaves will take 50 to 60 minutes.

Bake for slightly longer than you think is necessary. It should sound hollow when thumped, and the wonderful aroma should be filling your kitchen.

Minimal-Knead Sourdough Sandwich Bread

This makes four loaves of bread and uses 4 cups of starter. Refer to the "Caring for Your Sourdough Starter" section for information on building up your starter.

Remember to hold back at least ½ cup starter to keep your starter going.

It is easy to cut the recipe in half for two loaves or double it to make eight loaves. When doubling, you may need to use two bowls.

- 4 cups active starter, fed within the previous 6 to 12 hours
- 3 ½ cups buttermilk or kefir, or a combination of the two
- 1 ½ tablespoons sea salt
- ⅓ cup Sucanat or Rapadura★
- 3 tablespoons butter, melted
- 10 cups whole wheat or all-purpose flour, or 5 cups of each★

In a large bowl, mix together starter and buttermilk. Add salt, sweetener, and butter. Mix well.

Add flour 2 cups at a time, stirring with a wooden spoon to combine between additions. When the dough is too thick to mix with a wooden spoon, you can use your hands.

When you have 10 cups of flour added, give it a quick knead. You want the dough to be thick yet still shaggy. Spend only a minute or two kneading and combining all of the ingredients.

Butter the top of your bread and then give it a flip and butter the other side. Cover with a tea towel and set in a warm place.

Let it set and rise for 12 to 15 hours. I usually start my bread late afternoon and allow to rise overnight.

After the 12 to 15 hours, your dough should have risen a fair amount, probably not doubled but definitely larger. It'll also be light and airy. Get out your loaf pans and butter them generously.

Punch it down, then divide your dough into four pieces. Take one piece at a time and work it in your hands.

Push the bread into one of your buttered bread pans. Once you have it squished in, flip the dough over.

Repeat with each piece of dough. Cover your pans with a tea towel and allow a second rise. The second rise takes 4 to 8 hours depending on temperature.

When you're ready to bake, preheat the oven to 425°.

Bake for 15 minutes at 425°, then turn down to 325° for 35 to 45 minutes or until the bread is done. (If you turn the bread out and thump the bottom, it should sound hollow when fully baked.)

*Sucanat and Rapadura are unrefined sweeteners with a high molasses content. You could substitute honey, but since it is sweeter, use less (scant ¼ cup) and be aware you may need to use slightly more flour because of honey being a liquid. I've made this without any sweetener with great results.

*My favorite flour for this recipe is freshly ground hard red wheat. It gives a wonderful, almost nutty flavor. It also results in a dense loaf. If you're new to sourdough or whole wheat, try this with fresh ground hard white wheat or even regular all-purpose flour. Or use a combination of hard red wheat and hard white or all-purpose flour.

Swirl Loaf or Swirl Rolls

Be still, my heart! My simple Rustic Dough or Minimal-Knead Sandwich Bread dough puts on fancy airs with just a few alterations. Swirl Bread can be made savory or sweet depending on your mood. This is more of a method than a recipe. I'll share how I make my Cinnamon Swirl Bread and then give you a few ideas for other options.

- Mix the dough as instructed in Rustic Biscuits or Minimal-Knead Sourdough Sandwich Bread. Let it sit to sour for at least 6 hours.
- If you're using the Rustic Biscuits recipe *and* filling with a sweet filling, mix in 2 tablespoons to ½ cup of your favorite granulated sweetener. I prefer a natural cane sugar, such as Sucanat or Rapadura. The sandwich bread recipe already has sweetener, so there's no need to add additional. If you are making a savory swirl, you don't need a sweetener.
- Lightly flour a cutting board or section of your counter and roll the bread out. If you plan to bake your Swirl Loaf in a bread pan, keep the length of the pan in mind as your roll. If you're

doing a free-form loaf on a baking sheet, you won't need to worry as much. You want the dough about an inch or so thick. I roll mine into something resembling a rectangle, but it doesn't need to be exact.

- Generously butter the dough with about ¼ cup softened butter, keeping it ½ to ¾ of an inch from the edge. Once it's buttered, sprinkle with cinnamon sugar (¼ to ½ cup of Sucanat, or another dry sweetener, plus 1 tablespoon cinnamon mixed together). Then you can add raisins and/or nuts if you wish. Gently press everything down to secure.
- Now you are ready to roll.
- Start at the smallest edge and gently roll, being careful not to lose your filling. Cinnamon sugar stays in fairly well. If you use larger things (like crumbled cheese) you may have to be more careful.

Once it is rolled up, you have a decision to make.

Will you make a Swirl Loaf or Swirl Rolls?

Swirl Loaf: Carefully move your rolled-up dough to a well-buttered bread pan or leave it more free-form by moving it to a buttered baking sheet. Cover with a cloth and let rise for a couple of hours.

Preheat your oven to 425°. Bake for 15 minutes. Turn down to 325° and bake for 35 to 45 minutes until bread is done. It should sound hollow when thumped.

Remove from the oven and let rest at least 15 minutes before slicing.

Swirl Rolls: Butter an 8 x 8 baking dish. Once the dough is rolled up, very gently cut it into ½ to ¾ inch pieces. I use a serrated knife for this.

Move each cut piece to your buttered baking dish with the swirls facing up (think cinnamon rolls), allowing them to slightly touch. You want to be extremely careful so that your fillings stay in place.

Cover with a cloth and allow to rise for a couple of hours.

Bake at 325° for 30 minutes or until the rolls are no longer gooey. Remove from oven and allow to cool.

Sometimes I move them to a rack for cooling if they look like they are holding together well. If they look fragile, just leave them in the pan to cool. They should hold together better afterward. Serve warm or even allow to cool and add frosting to the sweet version.

Here are a few filling ideas. Whatever you add, be sure that you keep it about ½ to ¾ inch away from the edge of the dough so it doesn't all fall out in the rolling and baking steps.

- Butter and cinnamon sugar
- Butter, orange zest, and sugar
- Softened flavored coconut oil (you want it soft but not liquid), brown sugar, and coconut shreds or flakes
- Butter, brown sugar, and pecans (or your favorite nut)
- Cheddar cheese and crispy bacon bits (cooked and cooled)
- Mozzarella, sun-dried tomatoes (rehydrated and chopped small), fresh garlic, and fresh basil
- Mozzarella with pesto
- Cheddar cheese with fresh herbs
- Olive tapenade
- Parmesan cheese, sautéed mushrooms, and herbs

Sourdough French Toast with Nut and Fruit Syrup

Did you know French toast didn't originate in France? It's widely believed to have existed since the Roman Empire. Other sources say it was created during the Middle Ages. Wherever it originated, French toast is a tasty, frugal way to revive day-old bread. It's especially delicious with homemade syrup.

French Toast

- 1 loaf of sourdough bread, sliced thick or thin (your choice)
- 6 eggs
- ¾ cup milk
- ½ teaspoon cinnamon
- ½ teaspoon nutmeg
- 2 teaspoons honey (or another natural sweetener)

Combine eggs, milk, cinnamon, nutmeg, vanilla, and honey in a baking dish. (I often use a 9 x 13 pan, but any shallow dish will work.)

Place a single layer of bread in the egg mixture. Allow to set for 2 to 3 minutes on each side of the bread.

Meanwhile, heat your skillet or griddle to medium heat. Add a little ghee, coconut oil, or other healthy cooking fat.

Cook your egg-battered bread for about 4 minutes on the first side and 2 to 3 minutes on the second side until done to your liking.

Top with butter as the bread comes off the heat. Serve plain or with honey, maple syrup, yogurt, fruit or one of the nut and fruit syrups below.

Syrup

You can use any type of nut you have on hand for this syrup. I often use almonds or walnuts. Cashews also work well. I'm sure other types of fruit would also work; orange or mandarin segments would be terrific using the banana syrup method.

Apple and Nut Syrup

- 1 apple
- 1 cup nuts, roughly chopped
- ⅔ tablespoon butter
- ½ cup honey

Peel (or not) and chop apple into bite-size pieces.

Add apple pieces plus 2 tablespoons butter to a skillet and cook over medium heat until the apple begins to soften.

Add nuts and additional butter (if needed) and allow to cook for 2 to 3 minutes, stirring often to prevent burning.

Pour in honey and stir. The honey will melt, transforming into a beautiful syrup.

Serve warm over Sourdough French Toast, pancakes, etc. Or cool slightly and use as a topping for yogurt.

Banana and Nut Syrup

- 1 cup nuts, roughly chopped
- 2 tablespoons butter
- ½ cup honey
- 2 bananas

Combine nuts and butter in a skillet and cook over medium heat for 2 to 3 minutes.

Pour in honey and stir to coat. After the honey is completely melted, add the bananas and gently stir to mix.

Let cook for 1 to 2 minutes.

The honey will take on a delicious banana flavor. Serve warm over Sourdough French Toast, pancakes, etc. Or cool slightly and use as a topping for yogurt.

Almost-Instant Sourdough Pancakes

Soft in the middle, yet crispy and delicious on the outside. These Almost-Instant Sourdough Pancakes are a thrifty way to use your discarded sourdough starter! They go together super fast, making them just as quick and easy to use as a box mix. This recipe is adapted from Traditional Cooking School.

- 2 tablespoons butter or coconut oil, barely melted
- ¼ teaspoon sea salt
- 1 egg
- 1 tablespoon natural sweetener, such as honey, maple syrup, Sucanat, etc.
- ½ teaspoon vanilla extract (optional)
- 1 sprinkle cinnamon and/or nutmeg (optional)
- 1 cup sourdough starter, fed the night before (you can use your discard)
- ½ teaspoon baking soda
- 1 tablespoon water

Heat your favorite griddle or pancake-cooking skillet. While it's heating, whisk together butter, egg, sea salt, sweetener of choice, vanilla extract, and spices in a medium-sized bowl or a large measuring cup. I love using a large measuring cup since it allows me to easily pour the pancake batter onto the griddle.

Add your sourdough starter and stir well with a whisk. Set aside.

In a small cup, combine water and baking soda. Set aside.

Check your griddle. Is it ready? Add a little smear of butter or coconut oil to help with the cooking process.

Pour the water/baking soda mixture into your waiting pancake batter. Quickly stir to incorporate.

Pour or scoop the batter onto the griddle, using approximately ¼ cup for each pancake. Brown on both sides.

Serve hot with butter and syrup, or try my *Farmer Boy Pancakes* inspired by Laura Ingalls Wilder's book by the same name.

Farmer Boy Pancakes

As the pancakes come out of the skillet, slather each one with butter and then sprinkle ¼ to ½ teaspoon of Sucanat (or brown sugar) over each. The next pancake goes over the top and the process continues.

When serving, take a portion from the stack and top with yogurt, clabber cheese, or cottage cheese. Delicious!

Note: Get recipes for homemade yogurt and cheeses at HomespunOasis.com/Sourdough-Resources.

Almost-Instant Sourdough Focaccia Bread

This super quick and easy recipe is a great way to use your discarded sourdough starter! Adapted from Sourdough Pesto Pizza by Traditional Cooking School.

- 1 cup sourdough starter
- ½ teaspoon sea salt
- 1 teaspoon dried basil

Preheat oven to 400° Fahrenheit.

Grease a well-seasoned cast-iron skillet (10 or 12 inches) with avocado oil or oil of choice.

Place greased skillet in oven for 10 minutes to preheat.

While the skillet is heating, mix all ingredients in a 1-cup measuring cup.

Once preheated, remove skillet.

Pour sourdough batter directly into skillet.

Tip the skillet to swirl the starter and create a circular pizza shape. Spread the starter out, if necessary, with a spoon or spatula. The sourdough starter will start to cook immediately as the pan is scorching hot.

Immediately place the skillet back in the oven for an additional 6 to 10 minutes. Depending on how thin your crust is, it could take 6 minutes, 10 minutes, or somewhere in between.

Turn out on a plate (or leave in the skillet) and slice into wedges.

Variation: After the baking is done, top the focaccia bread with shredded cheese, sliced tomatoes, and fresh basil. Return to the oven for 3 or 4 minutes to melt the cheese.

Idea: This focaccia bread can double as a quick pizza crust. Adding pizza sauce will result in a soft crust, even with the prebaking. You can skip the sauce and use a layer of sliced tomatoes or accept you won't have a super crisp crust and eat it with a fork.

Almost-Instant Sourdough Crackers

Here's another excellent way to use up your discarded starter! You just might love them so much you find yourself building up your starter to make a triple batch. True story.

- ¾ cup sourdough starter
- 2 tablespoons butter, ghee, or coconut oil, melted and allowed to cool (or use olive oil)
- ¼ teaspoon sea salt
- 1 teaspoon dried basil
- ½ teaspoon dried parsley
- ½ teaspoon dried oregano
- ¼ teaspoon garlic powder
- Additional sea salt for sprinkling

Preheat oven to 325°. Line a baking sheet with parchment paper.

Mix the sourdough starter, healthy fat, sea salt, and spices in a bowl. (I like to use a 2-cup glass measuring container because it's easy pour.) Stir well to combine.

Pour the sourdough mixture onto the parchment paper. Use a rubber spatula, off-set spatula, or a butter knife to spread the sourdough batter into a thin, even layer.

Sprinkle with additional sea salt. A coarse salt is nice for this, but finely ground salt works well too.

Bake for 10 minutes. Remove from oven and score into cracker-sized squares with a knife or pizza cutter.

Return to oven and bake for an additional 20 to 40 minutes, maybe more depending on thickness.

Check at the 20-minute mark to evaluate. You want them beautiful and golden.

Using a spatula, turn the crackers. If the scoring didn't break them apart, you can do that as you turn them.

Add additional cooking time in 5 to 10 minute increments. The crackers tend to be thinner around the edges. I remove any that look done when I do my check.

Let cool completely on the parchment paper.

Sourdough Muffin Formula

These muffins are extremely adaptable! Be sure to read the Basic Sourdough Muffin Formula, then go to the details on how this method works.

Having an easy and adaptable method, using basic ingredients and then customizing to your own tastes, and using "add-ins" that are abundant or economical to you, is a great way to maximize your food dollars, reduce food waste, and keep your food budget under control.

Learning multiple methods is a great addition to your food storage plans. My book *Design a Dish* shares more methods to help you stop relying on recipes and to make the most of what you have on hand.

Let's design a sourdough muffin!

Required Ingredients

- **Grain:** Use 2 to 2 ½ cups whole wheat flour. Or substitute oatmeal, cornmeal, or rye flour for the whole wheat flour. One of my favorite combinations for sweet muffins is equal parts whole wheat flour and old-fashioned rolled oats.

- *Liquid:* 1 cup water, dairy milk, plant-based milk, or a combination. I also like half yogurt or kefir and half water. This combination makes super light and airy muffins.
- Sourdough Starter: Use ⅓ cup starter, fed within the last 6 to 8 hours.
- *Fat:* Use ¼ cup melted butter, coconut oil, ghee, or other traditional fat. Or you can substitute an all-natural nut butter for all or part of the fat. Another thing that works well is using a "wet addition" for all or part of the fat. For a savory muffin, olive oil or melted tallow or lard work well. I've even used melted and cooled bacon fat.
- Egg: Use 1 egg.
- *Sweetener:* Use up to ½ cup of a natural sweetener, such as Sucanat, Rapadura, honey, maple syrup, blackstrap molasses, evaporated cane juice, or a combination of any of these. Keep in mind that honey, maple syrup, and molasses are liquid. Use caution when using these in combination with other wet additions so your batter does not become overly wet. Honey is also sweeter than other options, so you need less to get the same sweetness. I've had excellent result using as little as 2 tablespoons of sweetener, especially when combined with additions that are on the sweet side. If making a savory muffin, use only 2 tablespoons or eliminate completely.
- *Sea Salt:* ½ teaspoon of sea salt.
- *Baking Soda:* Use ¾ teaspoon.

You could stop here and make your muffins *plain*. I've made plain muffins many times. They turn out great.

But one of the really fun things about a method like this is the ability to customize the muffins to items that you have on hand. No need to make a special trip to the store. Use up that lonely apple in the fruit bowl, leftovers hanging out in the fridge, puréed pumpkin stashed in the freezer, that over producing zucchini from the garden. You have options with this method! This is a great way to use up small amounts of leftovers.

Optional Additions

These can be used in any combination you wish. The total amount of optional additions should not exceed 1 ½ cups, with no more than ½ cup as a "wet addition."

- **Dry Additions:** Chopped Crispy Nuts (almonds, peanuts, pecans, walnuts), sunflower seeds, raisins, shredded coconut, cocoa powder, peanut flour, etc. These can be mixed and matched.
  If using a small seed, such as poppy or chia, limit to 2 tablespoons when using on their own or add that amount to other dry ingredients. *Note:* cocoa powder and/or peanut flour can help the texture if your batter is too thin.
- **Moist Additions:** Blueberries, chopped or shredded apple, freshly shredded zucchini, shredded carrots, citrus zest, chocolate chips or chunks, etc.
- **Wet Additions:** Pumpkin purée, applesauce, mashed banana, cottage cheese, cooked and mashed sweet potato, cooked and mashed carrot, frozen zucchini that has been thawed and drained, home-canned fruit that has been drained and cut in chunks, fruit juice (lemon, lime, or orange as a flavoring only).
- **Spices:** 1 to 4 teaspoons, depending on your preferences. Use one or a combination of cinnamon, nutmeg, ground ginger, cloves, grated orange peel, grated lemon peel, etc.

Note: When using wet ingredients, your batter can get quite thin. This could result in additional baking time. To help eliminate this, I keep the wet ingredients to no more than ½ cup per batch—unless my dough seems too thick. A wet addition is a great way to thin a too-thick dough.

Variations and Ideas

- *All-Natural Fruit Spreads:* Here is an idea for a nice change of pace. Fill muffin tins half full of plain batter. Add a teaspoon of fruit spread and then top with 2 more teaspoons of batter.
- *Savory Muffins:* These make a nice accompaniment to a simple soup dinner. Use only 2 tablespoons of sweetener or omit entirely. I've had excellent results using a combination of whole wheat flour and rye flour, or whole wheat flour and cornmeal (equal amounts). Excellent additions are ½ cup shredded cheese, a few strips of fried and crumbled bacon, 2 or 3 tablespoons of any or all of the following: minced or grated onion, shredded zucchini, finely chopped leftover cooked vegetables (I like broccoli), parmesan cheese, fresh herbs of your choice. If using dried herbs, use 1 to 2 teaspoons.

Tasty Combinations

After several years of designing our muffins, we've developed a couple favorites:

- *Lemon Poppy Seed:* When we want muffins or breakfast cake and I have nothing on hand that needs to be used up, I make a lemon poppy seed. My only additions are 2 tablespoons of poppy seeds, 2 tablespoons of lemon juice, 1 teaspoon each of ground cinnamon and ground ginger, and ½ teaspoon of nutmeg. Simple and delicious.
- *Peanut Butter Banana:* Bananas that are too ripe are very common here. (It seems I can never accurately estimate the banana consumption at my house. Either I buy too few and they're gone too quickly or too many and they become too ripe.) My additions then become overripe bananas and peanut butter. I usually replace half of the fat with the peanut butter to keep the batter from becoming too wet (so ⅛ cup peanut butter

and ⅛ cup of butter or coconut oil). This makes a very tasty combination.

Basic Sourdough Muffin Formula

Makes one dozen plus or minus.

Now that you're familiar with the components to muffins, here is your formula. Let the experiments begin!

I rarely make a single batch of muffins. I find it easier and more economical to make a double or even triple batch so we have muffins for a few days or to stash in the freezer.

Pro tip: Always use a larger bowl than you think you need.

- 2 to 2 ½ cups grain (flour, oatmeal, cornmeal, etc.; single grain or combination)
- 1 cup water or milk
- ⅓ cup sourdough starter

Combine your grain(s) with your liquid and sourdough starter. While I've found the above amounts result in an almost perfect dough (thicker than pancake batter and a little sticky), your grain choice may make your dough thinner or thicker.

If it's too thin, add additional flour a tablespoon at a time. If it's too thick, add milk or water a tablespoon at a time until you achieve a thick batter consistency.

Cover with a cloth and let sit at room temperature for 7 hours or overnight.

After your soaking time has completed, prepare your muffin tins. To your sourdough batter, add and mix well:

- Up to ¼ cup fat
- 1 egg

Note: After souring, your dough may be difficult to stir. I like using a wooden spoon to work it and break it up as I add the fat and egg. If you have bits of batter that didn't break up and incorporate into your mix, those bits will have a different texture and color. The muffins will still taste delicious.

In a separate bowl, combine:

- Up to ½ cup sugar
- ½ teaspoon salt
- Dry additions

Combine the two bowls until mixed, continuing to break up any hard bits that remained after adding the fat and egg.

Stir in any moist or wet additions.

When you are satisfied your batter is well combined, sprinkle with ¾ teaspoon baking soda and gently mix to combine.

Spoon into muffin tins. Bake in a 400° oven for 18 to 25 minutes. Your baking time may vary depending on your altitude and how wet your batter is.

Sourdough Breakfast Cake

Here's a great idea! Mix up your Sourdough Muffins and put the batter in an 8-inch square pan or a loaf pan and sell it to your family as "Breakfast Cake."

No need to wash each little muffin tin ;)

You'll need a 9 x 13 pan for a double batch.

Keep an eye on your quantity when pouring into pans. Sometimes your choice of ingredients can result in a batter that makes more than will fit in a pan without running over. Fill pans no more than ¾ full to be safe.

When batter exceeds the pan, put the remainder in muffin tins. Do you only have batter enough to fill a couple of tins? No problem! Putting water in the empty tins will aid in cooking and avoid burning.

Bake at 375° for 20 to 25 minutes for a single batch and 25 to 35 minutes for a double batch. As with the muffins, your baking time may vary depending on your altitude and how wet your batter is.

Sourdough Tortillas

These tortillas are soft, chewy, and pliable. The all-day soaking and souring not only aids in digestion but also breaks down some of the gluten to make rolling easier.

- ¾ cup water
- ¾ cup sourdough starter, fed within the last 6 to 12 hours
- ¼ cup olive oil (or coconut oil, butter, or ghee), plus additional oil for coating dough and frying
- ¾ teaspoon sea salt
- 3 cups whole wheat flour, or a combination of whole wheat and white flour

Souring Stage: Start at least 8 hours before you wish to begin rolling out your tortillas. You can sour for up to 24 hours, if necessary, but I like to put the dough in the fridge after 12 hours at room temperature.

Combine water, starter, oil, and salt. Use an electric mixer or mix by hand to incorporate.

Keep mixing and adding flour, ½ cup at a time, until the dough cleans the sides of the bowl and forms a ball in the center.

Mix and knead (either with a machine or by hand) until the dough holds together well and is somewhat pliable. This only takes a couple of minutes.

Oil your hands and generously coat the outside of the dough ball.

Cover with a damp towel or plastic wrap. Let rest for 8 hours or overnight.

Cooking Stage: After rest time is over, divide the dough into 16 parts for small tortillas or 12 parts for large ones.

Roll each part into a ball and put the balls back in the bowl. Cover the bowl to prevent the dough from drying out.

Heat a cast-iron skillet or griddle over medium heat. Add a small amount of oil to prevent sticking.

Add a small amount of flour to a flat work surface, such as a countertop.

With a lightly floured rolling pin, roll out one ball of dough into a circle that is approximately ⅛ inch thick, or your desired thickness. Don't worry if you can't make a perfect circle. It will still taste delicious!

Place the rolled-out tortilla on the skillet or griddle.

Let it cook for about 30 seconds or until there are several bubbles in the tortilla.

Flip the tortilla with a spatula and cook the other side for another 15 to 25 seconds, or until the bubbles are browned. Remove tortilla from pan and place between towels to stay warm and moist.

Roll out the next tortilla, adding additional flour as needed for rolling. Repeat until all of the balls have been rolled out and cooked. Add oil to pan as needed for cooking.

Store in a zip-top freezer bag in refrigerator or freezer.

Sourdough Flatbread

Using either my Rustic Biscuits dough or my Minimal-Knead Sourdough Sandwich Bread dough, I easily create a new bread option. This flatbread is a wonderful change of pace to regular bread and is a fabulous accompaniment to a curry or piping hot bowl of soup.

It's also super quick cooking and oven free—perfect for summertime meals. We even make this while camping! When camping or traveling, I don't bother with the rolling pin. I just press the dough out and make it as thin as I desire. The garlic can be omitted to use this as a sandwich wrap. Delicious!

The Method

Early in the day, mix up the dough for Rustic Biscuits or Minimal-Knead Sourdough Sandwich Bread. If you use the Minimal-Knead recipe, I use ¼ of the batch for flatbread and form the rest into loaves. The Rustic Biscuits recipe makes a smaller amount of dough, so I make the entire batch into flatbread and give us leftovers. You want to allow about 8 hours souring time until you are ready to cook.

When the souring time is completed, divide your dough as needed.

Mince three gloves of garlic (or use a heaping ¼ teaspoon of garlic powder) and work into the dough. Push and pull, kneading slightly while you work it in.

If the dough is overly sticky, feel free to add a small amount of flour, 1 tablespoon at a time. You want it to be a consistency that you can work with without it globbing onto your hands.

After the garlic is well distributed, divide your dough into little balls about the size of a golf ball. Cover with a cloth and let rise for 30 minutes or so.

Using a rolling pin and a little flour (if necessary) roll each ball into something resembling a circle. You want your flatbread slightly thicker than a tortilla shell. They will puff a small amount while cooking, so use your judgment as to how thin they should be.

Heat a cast-iron griddle or a couple of cast-iron skillets to medium. While these are heating, melt a couple tablespoons of butter in a saucepan.

When the skillet is hot, use a pastry brush to butter one side of the rolled dough. Put the buttered side down in the skillet and then butter the top. Allow the first side to cook about 2 minutes, then carefully flip and let the second side cook for a minute or two. Your flatbread should be a lovely golden brown.

Sourdough Fry Bread

Navajo Tacos with Sourdough Fry Bread is one of the all-time most popular recipes on my Homespun Oasis blog. The fry bread is a wonderful vehicle for containing all the delicious goodness of a chili-like sauce.

Though the focus of this book is sourdough, I give you my chili sauce recipe as a bonus so you can create the amazingness for yourself.

Sourdough Fry Bread also makes a sweet treat when drizzled with or dipped in honey. They reheat very well in the oven and fairly well in a skillet or toaster. Reheated bread can be slathered in butter and topped with your favorite jam or cinnamon sugar.

Sourdough Fry Bread

Start early morning or the night before.

- ½ cup sourdough starter
- 1 cup milk
- 2 ½ cups whole wheat flour
- ¼ teaspoon sea salt
- ¼ teaspoon baking soda
- Coconut oil, tallow, or your favorite fat for frying

Mix sourdough starter, milk, and flour until combined. Cover with a cloth and let sit for 7 to 24 hours.

When ready to fry, stir in sea salt. The dough will be fairly sticky and should stir easily. Don't overwork it, just get the salt in.

When the salt's mixed in, add baking soda and mix to combine. The baking soda will cause the dough to swell slightly.

To fry, in a large skillet or pan (I use a deep cast-iron one), heat about an inch of coconut oil, tallow, or your favorite traditional fat that can handle high heat.

While the oil is heating, shape your dough into patties, using flour as necessary to keep the dough from sticking to your hands. Your patties can be small enough to fit in the bottom of a soup bowl or large enough to fit on a plate. I find a 4- to 5-inch patty is the easiest size to work with.

When your oil is hot (a small piece of dough will sizzle), carefully put the patties in the oil to cook. Gently flip them over when they are brown on the bottom, about 2 minutes or so. Cook until brown on the second side.

Move to a cloth or paper towel covered dish and cover with a second cloth to keep warm while cooking the rest of the batch.

The Chili Sauce

This chili sauce is a great way to stretch a pound of ground meat. The addition of the beans and using the sauce on the fry bread results in a hearty meal.

Using broth, which is a protein sparer, also helps with the nutrition of this dish. A protein sparer helps your body use the protein it receives, reducing the amount of protein needed.

- ¼ to 1 pound of ground beef, chicken, turkey, or wild game
- Coconut oil or other healthy fat (if needed)
- 1 onion, diced
- 1 clove garlic, minced
- 2 to 3 cups cooked pinto beans with juice
- 1 (8-ounce) can tomato paste

- ½ to 1 cup beef broth (or water)
- Salt and pepper, to taste

In a cast-iron skillet, cook the beef and ½ of the onion (reserve the other half for taco topping). Add a little coconut oil or other healthy fat if needed when browning.

When the meat is mostly browned, add the garlic, beans, tomato paste, and ½ cup broth.

Let this mixture simmer for 30 minutes or so while you cook the fry bread, adding additional broth as needed. You want the chili to be on the saucy side. The fry bread will soak up the sauce and be amazingly delicious.

To Assemble

Put the fry bread on your plate. I love to break my bread up into pieces. My husband leaves his whole and cuts as he goes.

Add a ladle (more or less) of the chili. Top with lettuce, onions, tomatoes, cheese, salsa, sour cream, or anything else that you enjoy on your tacos.

Sourdough Corn Dog Muffins

A quick and easy lunch or snack. Reminds me of a day at the fair!

- ½ cup sourdough starter
- ¾ cup corn Masa Harina★
- 1 egg
- ½ teaspoon salt
- Up to ⅓ cup milk
- ½ teaspoon baking soda
- ¼ teaspoon garlic powder
- ¼ cup shredded cheese
- 1 tablespoon onion, finely minced
- 2 to 3 hot dogs, diced (I prefer Applegate Farms uncured beef or Hebrew National)

Mix together starter, Masa Harina, and egg. Add a little milk, just enough to achieve a cake batter consistency. Depending on the thickness of your sourdough starter, you may need less or more. I start with ¼ cup and add until the batter looks "right." Don't worry, this doesn't have to be exact!

Add baking soda and garlic powder and mix well. The baking soda will react with the sourdough, causing it to poof up, so be sure you've started with a large enough bowl.

Stir in cheese, onion, and then hot dogs.

Fill muffin tins almost to the top. These muffins do not rise. Bake for 18 to 25 minutes until the muffins test done.

*Masa Harina is sometimes called corn flour. Dried corn is soaked in slaked lime and then dehydrated.

Variation: Corn Dog Casserole

This muffin recipe easily turns into a casserole by doubling and cooking in a well-buttered cast-iron skillet. You will need to add additional cooking time.

Sourdough Pizza Crust

I originally found this recipe on a blog called Mommy's Soapbox (no longer available). I tweaked it slightly to fit our household needs.

This tasty pizza crust was a Friday night staple in my house when my youngest girls were teens. I'd start the crusts in the morning and let them sour all day, then we'd all join in the fun in the kitchen, rolling out dough, prepping toppings, and assembling while laughing.

As written, this makes two pizza crusts. It can easily be doubled or even tripled. The dough can be made ahead and frozen, or the crusts can be cooked and then frozen.

- 1 ½ cups sourdough starter, fed within the past 12 hours
- 2 cups whole wheat flour
- ½ teaspoon sea salt
- 2 tablespoons olive oil

Combine starter with flour. Cover and let rest for 7 to 24 hours.

About 3 hours before you wish to make your pizza, give your dough a stir and add the salt and olive oil.

Use your freshly washed hands to mix it. When you first add the salt and oil in, the texture will change. It may be slightly gummy. It will improve as you knead.

Continue kneading for 5 to 10 minutes until the dough is smooth and elastic. Cover and let rise for about 2 hours.

Preheat oven to 375°.

Divide the dough into two balls and let rest for 15 minutes.

Press into pans (I usually use a combination of pressing and my rolling pin).

Add your favorite toppings and bake for 10 to 15 minutes until toppings are bubbly and crust is golden.

Sourdough Pockets

Here's a quick and easy make-ahead lunch idea! This is inspired by the Empanadas from *Nourishing Traditions* by Sally Fallon.

Dough

Use the pizza dough, Rustic Biscuits dough, tortilla dough, or a portion of the Minimal-Knead Sourdough Sandwich Bread dough. Allow the dough to soak and sour for at least 7 hours.

Filling

When you're close to the end of the dough soaking and souring time, prepare your filling.

Filling options are limitless! You could sauté some veggies and add a little leftover chicken or other protein. Maybe make a pizza version stuffed with pepperoni, mozzarella cheese, and pizza sauce. Yum! Or how about a Mexican style with taco spiced meat and shredded cheddar?

Here's a simple beef and cabbage filling—a little like Bierocks—that we like:

- ½ pound ground beef, chicken, or wild game
- ½ onion, minced
- 3 green bell peppers, chopped
- ½ small head of cabbage, shredded
- Salt and pepper, to taste

Cook the beef and minced onion in a cast-iron skillet. When meat is browned, add peppers and cabbage. Cook until soft. Finish with salt and pepper to taste.

While your filling is cooking, form your dough into balls—larger than golf balls but not quite baseballs.

How many? You'll need to judge based on the amount of filling you're making and how many servings you want. One ball equals one Sourdough Pocket. (Use your leftover dough for biscuits, flatbread, or even donuts.)

Using a rolling pin and a dusting of flour, roll into circular shapes. Don't worry if they aren't perfect.

Assemble

Now comes the fun part! Take a dough circle and lay it out. Put a little filling off center (¼ to ⅓ of a cup, depending on size of your circle). Then pull the top of the dough over.

Use a fork to crimp the edges and seal the dough together (you may need to flour the fork to prevent sticking). Place on a buttered cookie sheet.

Repeat until all of your circles are made into filled pockets.

Bake

Bake at 375° for about 10 minutes, then flip each pocket over and bake an additional 8 to 10 minutes until golden. (My altitude is around 5,000 feet, so you may need to cook slightly more or less.)

Mmm…so good! And so easy and portable. These make fabulous lunches. They can be wrapped and frozen for future use.

Bierock Sourdough Pie

Inspired by Bierocks, this savory pie is a winner.

The first time I made this for my guys, they turned their nose up. I'll admit, it's not much to look at! But the first bite won them over. My son liked it so much, he had not only seconds but called dibs on the last piece for his afternoon snack!

I love this savory pie not only because it's delicious, but it is so simple.

For the filling:

- ½ pound ground beef, chicken, turkey, pork, or wild game
- ½ onion, diced
- ½ teaspoon sea salt
- ¼ teaspoon black pepper
- 3 cups shredded cabbage (about ¼ of a medium head)

Preheat oven to 400°. In a 10-inch cast-iron skillet, cook the ground meat with the onion. When the onions are translucent and the meat is nearly done, drain off any excess fat.

Return to heat and add salt and pepper. Stir to mix, then add the cabbage. I find adding half and letting it cook down a few minutes before adding the rest keeps me from having cabbage all over the floor.

Once all the cabbage is in the skillet, let cook for 5 minutes while you prepare the dough.

For the dough:

- 1 ½ cups sourdough starter, fed within the last 12 hours
- 3 eggs

- 1 teaspoon sea salt
- 1 teaspoon basil
- ½ teaspoon baking soda

In a bowl or 4-cup glass measuring cup, combine the starter, eggs, salt, and basil.

When your filling has cooked down, sprinkle the baking soda over the top and then stir vigorously.

Give the filling a final stir, smooth the top, and then turn off the heat. Pour the sourdough mixture over the top of the filling.

Move the skillet to the oven. Bake for 25 minutes or until cooked through.

Sourdough Donuts or Fritters

I started thinking about making these when reading one of the books from Lauraine Snelling focused on the people of Blessing, North Dakota. In the book, they have bread out to rise and decide to "steal" some of the dough to turn into a treat to have with their coffee.

I had a huge ah-ha moment. It's a rare day I don't have some sort of dough available. Could we have donuts at a moment's notice using this idea?

Over the years, I've made these with a variety of different doughs. This is not a recipe exactly, but more of an idea for you to adapt for your needs.

The Dough:

This can be just about anything! My Rustic Biscuit dough, Minimal-Knead Sourdough Sandwich Bread dough, Tortilla dough, and Fry Bread dough all work beautifully. Yeast bread dough is also an option.

How much dough you need depends on how many donuts you want to end up with.

When making a snack-sized amount of donut holes, a cup or so is enough for four servings.

If doing the Apple Fritter variation as a breakfast, use a bread loaf size amount for four generous fritters. Scale up or down to suit your needs.

Plain, untopped donuts can be stored in the fridge for later. If you add a topping, fresh is best.

The Sweetener:

When using sourdough, I like to add a bit of natural sweetener. My preference is Sucanat or Rapadura. These are dry, less-processed natural sweeteners. You can certainly use any dry sweetener you prefer. For each cup of dough, I add up to 1 tablespoon of dry sweetener.

Honey or maple syrup can be used as well, but since it's liquid, it can change the texture of the dough. If using a liquid sweetener, you may need additional flour.

If I'm using a dough that already contains sweetener, such as my Minimal-Knead dough, I either lessen the amount of additional sweetener or don't add any extra.

Spices:

I add cinnamon and nutmeg to the dough, somewhere around 1 teaspoon of cinnamon and ½ teaspoon of nutmeg per cup of dough.

You could try other spices too. Think about the spices you might use in muffins. Maybe a chai flavor with cardamon, allspice, cinnamon, cloves, and ginger? Adding cocoa powder to make chocolate donuts is also wonderful. Chocolate and sourdough, along with a dash of vanilla, is a beautiful combination.

Or don't add spices and just focus on toppings. The varieties are endless!

Baking Soda:

I use ½ teaspoon baking soda for each cup of dough after everything else has been worked in. Baking soda will help lighten the dough. It also sweetens and brings out the natural flavor of the sourdough and helps to remove excess tang.

Combine:

Put your dough in a bowl, add your sweetener and spices, then mix to combine. Depending on your dough's thickness, you may use a wooden spoon or your hands. If using your hands, knead to combine. After all is mixed well, sprinkle on your baking soda and mix again.

Fry:

I use a deep cast-iron skillet and unflavored coconut oil or a mild tallow. This is a shallow fry; you only need about an inch of oil. Heat until a small piece of dough sizzles when dropped in. Be sure to keep your heat around medium, and do not allow your oil to smoke.

For donut holes, I form the dough into a ball. I'm not exact with this, and depending on the dough's consistency, it is sometimes easier to carefully drop by teaspoons.

Allow it to cook a few minutes and then carefully turn over. I cook these very much like frying meatballs, rotating them to get each side. Again, watch your heat so it isn't too hot but is still hot enough to sizzle.

If I want to make a flat donut, I shape and then cook them somewhat like pancakes. A few minutes on side one, flip to side two and cook a few minutes, then back to side one to make sure it cooks through.

I haven't tried rolling out the dough and putting a hole in the center like an actual donut, but that might work well with a thick enough dough.

Your cooking oil can be strained and saved for your next batch of donuts!

Top 'Em:

As soon as the donuts are done and come out of the oil, I often roll them in cinnamon sugar. This is a combination of powdered Sucanat and cinnamon (whirl the Sucanat in a blender to make it powdered).

Other topping options include glaze, frosting, nuts, jam or jelly, sprinkles…just about anything! You could even dip the donuts in honey. Plain or fancy, there are so many options.

The Donut Formula:

If you've read my book *Design a Dish,* you know I'm a fan of formulas. A formula helps me stretch my food dollars by using ingredients that I have on hand or that are abundant to me to create tasty dishes and treats. My donut formula is very basic. Use the notes above, and feel free to adapt as you see fit!

- Dough of your choice (about 1 cup to make a snack-sized treat for four people)
- Natural sweetener
- Spices
- ½ teaspoon baking soda per 1 cup of dough
- Coconut oil for light frying
- Cinnamon sugar, glaze, frosting, nuts, jam, sprinkles, etc. for decorating (optional)

Combine dough, sweetener, and spices. Once well mixed, sprinkle baking soda on top and quickly work in.

Allow to rest while the oil heats. You want the oil hot enough to sizzle a small piece of dough. Form donuts into desired shape and gently fry until cooked through.

Roll in cinnamon sugar, frost, or serve plain for a tasty treat.

Variation: Apple Fritter

- 2 apples, cubed
- Healthy fat for cooking apples
- Dough of your choice
- Natural sweetener, such as Sucanat or honey
- Spices, such as cinnamon and nutmeg
- ½ teaspoon baking soda
- Coconut oil for light frying
- Cinnamon sugar or glaze (optional)

Cook apples in healthy fat until soft. Follow remaining directions above, forming into free-form patties—somewhat like the fritters you see in a donut shop. Sprinkle with cinnamon sugar or glaze.

Sourdough Banana Cake

Sourdough Cake? Don't mind if I do!

This cake is moist and delicious and not at all sour. Not a fan of bananas? Be sure to check out the variations. There are sooo many options for this tasty cake.

This makes a 9 x 13 pan, but feel free to half the recipe for an 8 x 8 square.

- 2 cups whole wheat flour
- 1 cup sourdough starter, fed within the last 12 hours
- ½ cup milk, water, or combination
- ½ to 1 cup Sucanat, Rapadura, or other natural sugar
- ½ cup barely melted butter, coconut oil, or ghee
- 3 very ripe medium bananas, mashed
- 1 teaspoon vanilla extract
- 3 eggs
- 1 teaspoon sea salt
- 1 teaspoon ground cinnamon
- 1 teaspoon ground cloves
- ½ teaspoon allspice
- ¾ teaspoon baking soda
- ¾ teaspoon baking powder

Combine starter, milk, and flour. Cover and let soak/sour at room temperature for at least 7 hours and up to 24 hours.

Preheat oven to 350°. Grease a 9 x 13 pan, or two 8" or 9" square or round pans. Sprinkle with flour and set aside.

In a separate mixing bowl, combine sweetener, oil, mashed banana, vanilla, and eggs. Mix to combine.

Add sourdough mixture, salt, spices, baking soda, and baking powder. Beat until smooth. If the batter seems a little thick, add additional milk or water, 1 tablespoon at a time.

Pour into prepared pan(s). Bake for 35 to 45 minutes or until it tests done (smaller pans may cook quicker). A toothpick or fork inserted in the center should come out clean.

Remove from oven and set on a rack to cool. This can be allowed to fully cool and frosted (dark chocolate frosting is amazing with banana cake) or served warm and plain.

Store leftovers in the fridge.

Variations

- Simple and Delicious Sourdough Spice Cake: Double the amount of oil and omit the mashed bananas. Proceed with recipe as written.
- Sourdough Carrot Cake: Double the amount of oil and omit the mashed bananas. Add 2 cups grated carrots, ½ cup crushed pineapple (drained), ¼ to ½ cup finely chopped walnuts, and ¼ cup unsweetened shredded coconut. Proceed with recipe as written. Carrot cake, of course, needs cream cheese frosting.
- Sourdough Pumpkin Cake: Substitute 1 ½ cups puréed pumpkin (or squash) for the bananas. Add ½ teaspoon nutmeg and ½ teaspoon ground ginger. Proceed with recipe as written. A dusting of powdered sugar is nice on this.
- Applesauce Spice Cake: Substitute 1 ½ cups applesauce (smooth or chunky) for the bananas. Proceed with recipe as written.
- Chocolate Applesauce Spice Cake: Substitute 1 ½ cups applesauce (smooth or chunky) for the bananas. Add ⅓ cup cocoa powder and ¼ cup raisins (optional). Proceed with recipe as written.

- Sourdough Zucchini Cake: Do you have garden zucchini coming out your ears? Sourdough Zucchini Cake to the rescue! Double the amount of oil and omit the mashed bananas. Add 2 cups grated zucchini (squeeze out excess moisture), 1 teaspoon lemon zest (optional), ¼ to ½ cup finely chopped walnuts or pecans, and ¼ cup golden raisins (optional, or use regular raisins). Proceed with recipe as written.

Sourdough Croutons or Breadcrumbs

Looking for a great way to revive an older loaf of sourdough? Croutons to the rescue!

Croutons or breadcrumbs can be as simple as cubing your loaf of bread (a ½ inch dice is about perfect) and then dehydrating until crispy. Depending on your dehydrator and the size of your cubes, this could take 2 to 5 hours.

If you don't have a dehydrator, you can use your oven set to the lowest temp. I also leave the door cracked open to allow a little of the heat to escape. Keep a close eye on the croutons so they don't burn.

Use the croutons on soups or salads, just like you would use any crouton, or whirl the cubes in the blender to make breadcrumbs that are perfect for salmon patties, meatloaf, casseroles, etc.

If you prefer seasoned croutons or breadcrumbs, try this recipe:

- 1 loaf of bread, cubed
- 2 tablespoons dried parsley
- 2 tablespoons dried oregano
- 2 teaspoons sea salt
- 2 teaspoons garlic powder
- 1 teaspoon onion powder
- 1 teaspoon black pepper
- ½ cup melted butter, ghee, unflavored coconut oil, or lard

Combine seasonings in a small bowl and mix well. Set aside.

In a separate larger bowl, add your diced bread cubes and drizzle half of the warm, melted fat over the top. Sprinkle on half of the seasoning mix. Use a pair of wooden spoons or tongs to toss and lift the bread cubes, coating with the fat and seasonings. Add the rest of the fat and seasoning, then toss again.

Dehydrate in your dehydrator or oven as instructed above and then blend for breadcrumbs.

Note: Instead of a full loaf of bread, you can use ½ to ¾ of a loaf to get slightly more seasoned croutons or breadcrumbs. The ingredients can be scaled up or down as desired.

Resources

Check out the Resources page that goes along with this book for more recipes, information, and helpful tools:

HomespunOasis.com/Sourdough-Resources

Find more sourdough information and recipes on my website:

HomespunOasis.com/Sourdough

Also by Millie Copper

Sprouts for Your Food Storage: Add Nutrition and Variety to Your Diet

Want to make delicious, healthy sprouts that your whole family will love?

Sprouts For Your Food Storage will show you how! Sprouts are an easy, cheap, and tasty vegetable anyone can grow. They require little space and can be done without any special equipment. Because the original product grows during the sprouting process, this is a great way to stretch a small amount into a larger amount.

Real Food Hits the Road: Budget-Friendly Tips, Ideas, and Recipes for Enjoying Real Food Away from Home

Are you planning to hit the road for a family vacation? Do you want to take a road trip, but the idea of eating out three meals a day doesn't work for your budget or your health?

Real Food Hits the Road will be your guide to saving the budget, keeping your digestion working well, and eating real food away from home while letting you enjoy the trip and not "cook" all of the time.

Stock the Real Food Pantry: Save Money and Time While Gaining Peace of Mind

Do you want to stock your pantry with nutritious food your family will actually eat? In these trying times, are you focusing on your food storage?

If so, *Stock the Real Food Pantry* has you covered. Learn how a wonderfully stocked real food pantry will save you money and time—while giving you peace of mind.

Design a Dish: Save Your Food Dollars!

Would you like to learn great methods to reduce food waste? What if you could enjoy one meal for "free" each week?

Design a Dish will teach you how to make wonderful, simple dishes you can prepare day in and day out. You'll be amazed at how easy it is to nourish your family with these tasty dishes!

Stretchy Beans: Nutritious, Economical Meals the Easy Ways

Do you struggle with feeding your family delicious, healthy meals? Are you tired of trying to figure out what's for dinner each night? Do you cringe when you see how much money your family spends on groceries each month?

If so, *Stretchy Beans* is the solution you've been looking for! Learn how to easily prepare dinners that the whole family will love—while staying on budget, spending less time in the kitchen, and not losing your sanity.

About the Author

Millie Copper, writer of Cozy Apocalyptic Fiction and preparedness mentor, was born in Nebraska but never lived there. Her parents fully embraced wanderlust and moved regularly, giving her an advantage of being from nowhere and everywhere.

As an adult, Millie is fully rooted in a solar-powered home in the wilds of Wyoming with her husband and young son, milking ornery goats and tending chickens on their small homestead. In their free time, they escape to the mountains for a hike or laze along the bank of the river to catch their dinner. Four adult daughters, three sons-in-law, and three grandchildren round out the family.

Since 2009, Millie has authored articles on traditional foods, alternative health, homesteading, and preparedness—many times all within the same piece. Millie has penned five nonfiction, traditional food focused books, sharing how, with a little creativity, anyone can transition to a real foods diet without overwhelming their food budget.

The twelve-installment *Havoc in Wyoming* Christian Post-Apocalyptic fiction series uses her homesteading, off-the-grid, and preparedness lifestyle as a guide. The adventure continues with the *Montana Mayhem* series.

Find Millie at www.MillieCopper.com
Facebook: www.facebook.com/MillieCopperAuthor/
Amazon: www.amazon.com/author/MillieCopper
BookBub: https://www.bookbub.com/authors/Millie-Copper

www.ingramcontent.com/pod-product-compliance
Lightning Source LLC
Chambersburg PA
CBHW071216120626
46546CB00006B/2595